what's your excuse
for not being more
confident

what's your excuse ...

BEING MORE CONFIDENT?

Overcome your excuses, increase your confidence, unleash your potential

charlotta hughes

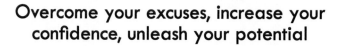

"This terrific book is packed full of insights and eureka moments that will help build the confidence of even the most self-doubting reader. It's easy to read, and the many exercises and tips are easy to follow and adopt, leaving us with no excuses for not feeling as confident as possible!"

Martin Clark, Editor OM Magazine

"I am not new to self-improvement books but found this concise, well-written book quite special. A reminder that confidence is at the root of making any change to your life and the excuses were all too familiar. Really good practical suggestions to take forward and this is a book I will share with many friends"

Tamara Hanton, Head of HR, Public Sector

"Charlotta helps people find practical, achievable ways to be the best possible version of themselves. I would strongly endorse her for her warmth, positivity and her insight into human nature. She has fantastic, natural communication skills and empathy and takes a genuine, deep interest in people. She challenges preconceptions and helps people to analyse situations clearly"

Megan Jenkins, Law Firm Manager

"This book is fantastic. It's like having a one-to-one life coaching session with Charlotta, personally tackling each excuse for low self-esteem. I suspect most of us will have used the excuses in this book at some point to sabotage our own success. I really liked the approachable, down to earth solutions that Charlotta succeeds in presenting so well. Each tip and tool enables new thinking to emerge to change those deeply ingrained habits. I shall be thoroughly recommending it to friends and patients who struggle with confidence and self-esteem"

Dr Sam Powell, GP

"Brilliant, brilliant, brilliant! Thank you for enabling me to see that our hurdles in life are really self-constructed. If we can accept that, we give ourselves the power to change and control our lives"

Karen Mercer, Owner of My Coffee Stop

"I am now less fearful of the future as I know that I am in control of my own happiness and that I am worthy of whatever I want to do or achieve. I now trust and believe in myself more"

Emma Cowell, Founder Astuto Design

"Charlotta writes with such warmth and enthusiasm that it's impossible not to feel inspired by her words. It even felt like Charlotta was right there in the room with me, encouraging me along. She first offers the tools to understand confidence and then helps you to start rebuilding your own, step by step. It is an essential read for anyone who has felt a lack of confidence at any time in their life."

Anne-Marie Sanderson, North London News

Also in this series

What's Your Excuse for not....

Living a Life You Love?
Getting Fit?
Loving Your Job?
Eating Healthily?
Being Better with Money?

What's Your Excuse for not Being More Confident?

This first edition published in 2017 by WYE Publishing
9 Evelyn Gardens, Richmond TW9 2PL
www.wyepublishing.com

Copyright © Charlotta Hughes 2017

Charlotta Hughes asserts her moral right to be identified as the
author of this book

ISBN 978-0-9933388-8-5

Printed and bound in Great Britain by
Marston Book Services Ltd, Oxfordshire

Cover and text design by Annette Peppis & Associates

'What's Your Excuse…?' is a UK Registered Trade Mark
(Registration No: 3018995)

www.whatsyourexcuse.co.uk
Follow What's Your Excuse…? on Twitter – @whats_yr_excuse
www.facebook.com/whatsyourexcusebooks

www.bemelifecoaching.com
www.facebook.com/bemelifecoaching.com
Follow Charlotta on Twitter – @CharlottaHughes
Follow Charlotta on Instagram – charlottahughes

Contents

Introduction

How to use this book

Whether you've struggled with poor self-confidence for as long as you can remember or if something has happened more recently to knock your confidence, this book is designed to help you take charge and improve how you feel about yourself and your life.

As a life coach specialising in confidence I have helped a large number of individuals find and increase their own self-confidence in ways that many of them hadn't thought possible. Often this work involves identifying and dispelling the beliefs my clients hold about themselves and their lives. This enables them to take control of how they feel, giving them the power to improve things and to enjoy their lives and their progress – whether at work, in study or privately.

The beliefs people hold about themselves often surface as excuses and in my work I hear variations of the same excuses for not feeling confident time and time again. In fact I used to use some of them myself, which is one of the reasons I'm so passionate about helping my clients to tackle their own. This book is a compilation of all of the excuses I've come across over the years, with suggestions and tips on how to address and overcome them.

The fact is that we all, at times, have excuses for why we don't feel how we'd like, or achieve or have the things we'd like, and the annoying thing with us humans is that we do whatever it takes to prove ourselves right. Even if the only person we hurt in the process is ourselves! You may well be able to reel off a list of what feel like perfectly legitimate reasons for why you have, and perhaps *should* have, poor confidence.

It may sound confrontational to say that you're making excuses, because with an emotion like confidence your excuses will feel like real, justifiable *reasons*. But however justified you think you are, if you acknowledge that these 'reasons' are in fact functioning as excuses you give yourself the opportunity to tackle them so that you can increase your confidence. This is not about belittling how you feel but instead about liberating yourself from your limiting beliefs.

To be confident may not feel like a choice or even an option right now, but the great news is that you have more ability to improve your confidence levels than you may realise. And this book will help.

You may want to read the book cover to cover and absorb all the positive messages throughout, to identify which excuses are true for you and then use the tips and techniques which most resonate with you to tackle them. Alternatively, you may use it as a reference guide and dip into the chapters that are relevant at certain times, to take control of your circumstances and emotions as and when you need to.

And if you find yourself coming up with excuses not covered in this book I would love to hear from you and I'll incorporate them in future editions!

The benefits of being more confident

A high level of self-confidence positively impacts on all areas of your life – at work, study or home and in social situations. It allows you to be more *you,* and to be the best version of you. Imagine the relief of just knowing that whatever happens and whatever the outcome you'll be fine, and that if you don't get the results you hoped for you'll be able to handle it and find a different way to get there.

Confident people tend to be more optimistically minded, which results in them not only making the most of opportunities but also in them expecting a positive outcome, which increases the likelihood of that outcome materialising. And, importantly, their confidence allows them to enjoy the process more. So a real three-way win – with confidence you take more chances, enjoy taking them and enjoy more frequent success!

Having self-confidence does not mean that you can do everything. Self-confident people have expectations that are realistic, but even when their expectations are not met, they continue to be positive and to accept themselves.

The benefits of having solid self-confidence are huge, and include:

- Greater happiness
- Greater peace of mind
- Better health
- Better relationships
- Less stress
- Improved performance
- More resilience
- The ability to be kinder to yourself
- A more positive outlook
- Improved social life
- Better balance across your life
- Greater feeling of control
- Less vulnerability to setbacks and criticism
- Better decision making skills
- The ability to know what you want
- Feeling more comfortable with risk
- Feeling more attractive
- Greater creativity
- More openness to opportunities
- More personal and professional success

A Managing Director of a major corporation once said to me: 'Success is less related to intelligence than it is to levels of confidence'.

So if you are holding yourself back based on a perception of your own shortcomings, each of those shortcomings is likely to be less relevant than your level of confidence. Find a way to tackle your excuses, act and feel confident, and the success, enjoyment and fun will follow.

The consequences of lacking confidence

The impact of a lack of confidence on you and the progression of your life is huge. It can spoil your greatest achievements and what would otherwise be your happiest moments. In fact it can even prevent them from happening. This could be due to a tendency to put yourself and everything you do down, so that you don't recognise or celebrate your successes. Or it could be due to your not achieving things in the first place because your insecurities interfere with your performance, or because you don't even allow yourself to try.

Either way the importance of confidence to your life and how it evolves cannot be underestimated.

If you lack confidence, these are some of the things you may experience:

- More susceptibility to stress
- Anxiety
- Poor sleep
- More physical ailments and illnesses
- Slower progress towards goals

- Less success
- Unrealised potential
- Unhappiness
- Depression
- Nervousness
- Poor relationships
- Missed opportunities
- Feelings of being hurt or undermined
- Inability to understand what you're good at
- Lack of motivation
- Poor self-image
- A lack of understanding of what you want or what you enjoy

Find ways to develop your own self-confidence and your mental and physical wellbeing are likely to improve as a consequence, along with an improved perception of your own quality of life. And few things are more important to us than that!

The definition of confidence

According to the Cambridge Dictionary the definition of confidence is, 'The quality of being certain of your abilities or of having trust in people, plans, or the future'.

What confidence means to *you* will be very personal, and if you feel that you haven't got enough, the definition is likely to be more about what you perceive to be lacking in yourself or your life than about what you feel already exists or is good.

In order to address and improve feelings of poor confidence, it's important to be clear about what your own personal definition looks like. Many of my coaching clients arrive at coaching with a clear desire for greater confidence but, sometimes surprisingly to themselves, a rather vague picture of what that greater confidence would look and feel like for them. Use the excuses included in this book to help you identify your own weaknesses and to improve *your* self-confidence.

The Excuses

Fears

I'm scared of failure

Are you avoiding going after what you really want because you're scared of failure, and the associated feelings of rejection, disappointment and embarrassment? The fact is, if you don't try, you guarantee failure.

In fact, not trying is the *only* way to guarantee failure. So you may spare your own feelings ('it's not my fault, I didn't even try'), but you won't ever have that thing you want. Which will reinforce your feelings of self-doubt. Doesn't really make sense, does it?

Another similar line of thinking is, 'I'll go for it with confidence when I'm ready'. What you're really likely to be saying to yourself is, 'I'll go for it when I can be sure I'll succeed'. But the question is, can you ever actually *know* you'll succeed?

> The fact is, if you don't try, you guarantee failure

Upon reflection, you'll probably agree that seeking such guarantees encourages the type of failure mentioned above. Failure caused by the absence of trying.

If you recognise that this is true for you challenge

yourself when these thoughts come upon you – 'how can I know I won't succeed at something I've not yet done?' As Pippi Longstocking the children's book character says, 'I have never tried that before, so I think I should definitely be able to'.[1] Lovely attitude, and if you'd like to adopt it, why not place a note of it on your fridge door or type it onto your screensaver to act as a regular reminder? In fact, one of the best ways to gain self-confidence is to do what you're afraid or nervous about.

If you set yourself a clear target and go for it you are much more likely to get nearer that target than if you didn't have a specific one in mind. So you may not succeed 100% but you'll get closer, which has to be better than being stuck in a rut and feeling unfulfilled. To illustrate: if you set your target at 10, you would be much more likely to reach an 8 than if you didn't have a target. So the 8 wouldn't be a failure as it would be a lot more than the 4 or 5 you might reach without proper focus. You can apply these numbers to any scenario you like – number of people to meet at an event, amount you'll earn or save in the next year, weight you'll lose in the

> I have never tried that before, so I think I should definitely be able to

---

1   Astrid Lindgren, *Pippi Longstocking*, Puffin, 2005

next month, number of dates you'll go on during a certain period of time and so on.

Extreme, black-and-white thinking means that you don't allow yourself the chance of, say, a 60% improvement due to a fear of not achieving 100%. For anything to be 100% successful, right or good it would need to be perfect, and perfection is a pretty unattainable goal. So such polarised thinking really does set you up to fail and reinforces that feeling of insecurity and lack of confidence.

Related to this can be the desire to be guaranteed a great future, and by seeking this guarantee, essentially about an unknown quantity, you may be causing yourself paralysis in the present. Reframe the unhelpful 'perfect future' scenario by telling yourself that the future is never actually here. By virtue of being the future it's always ahead of you. Lots of todays will all add up to your future and eventually to your past. So focus on the here and now. The best way to strive for a great future is by making every day in the present count.

Instead of allowing the fear of failure to get in your way, overcome procrastination by setting your target and going for it.

See more on the benefits of goal setting in "I'm an underachiever", see more on how to live in the present in "I have too much on my plate" and find out how to reduce the impact of your fears in "My fears are stupid!".

I'm scared I might succeed

If fear of failure is one side of a coin, fear of success is the other.

Do you ask yourself, 'What if I achieve my goal? Can I really handle it?' Do you think it may ultimately result in failure because you're not up to it, so probably best to avoid it in the first place? You could argue that the fear of success ultimately is about a fear of failure too.

You may be unaware of these thoughts but act in accordance with them anyway. So you find excuses and reasons why you cannot do things, why something would be a bad idea and so on. Alternatively you might find you forget or diarise the wrong date or time of an important meeting or event – an 'accidental' avoidance technique driven by your subconscious.

Here are some examples to demonstrate how fear of success can prevent progress:

* Sally gets a great sales lead at work and finds all manner of excuses not to pick up the phone because deep down she is thinking, 'What if I get the deal? Could I handle the workload/expectations/ success?'

* Harry is avoiding asking for a date. 'What if she says yes and then I'll have to impress her for a whole

evening. She'll probably come away thinking I'm boring. Best not to ask in the first place!'

* Claire is sabotaging her chances of losing weight because if she loses the weight people might notice her more. She is hiding behind the extra pounds. She has a perception that slim equals confidence and struggles to get over her insecurities about adopting a slim, fit person's attitude

Only when you allow yourself to examine your own reasoning and behaviour can you do something about it. Once you realise how you're holding yourself back by trying to avoid the fear, do as the late Susan Jeffers said, 'Feel the fear and do it anyway' because the bottom line is that fears will always exist, they grow in magnitude when we try to control or avoid them and the only way to get rid of a fear is to go out and do what you're afraid of.[2] The 'doing it' has to come *before* you start feeling self-confident in a given situation. Until then, the only thing getting in your own way is you!

Also see "My fears are stupid!" for more on how to reduce the impact of your fears.

---

2   *Susan Jeffers, Feel the Fear and Do it Anyway, Vermilion, 2007*

I don't like change

Does change feel uncomfortable and make you anxious? Perhaps you find the unknown difficult or scary because it's unpredictable?

Is a feeling of being in control important to you? Do you need to know what's coming next?

In fact fear of change and fear of losing control are two sides of the same coin.

The truth is that life *is* unpredictable and by trying to control things you can easily end up increasing rather than decreasing your anxiety levels. This happens when you are trying to remain within your comfort zone because, though the comfort zone can be helpful and feel safe, when it keeps you stuck it's in fact very far from comfortable or helpful.

Therefore, your comfort zone is currently supporting your lack of confidence and in order to grow and develop your confidence, you need to push the boundaries of that zone.

Yet, do you find yourself resisting? Are you now thinking of a hundred reasons why you shouldn't change, why any attempts to change would fail or why making the change is too overwhelming or difficult?

Perhaps you talk about the change, think about it regularly and dwell on the reasons why you need the change but can't progress towards it? I bet that feels pretty frustrating!

If you think about it, your attempts to stay in control and within your comfort zone aren't helping, and you're actually getting in your own way, denying yourself the chance of more happiness in life.

Below is a list of ways in which you can help introduce change into your life and find the courage to step outside your comfort zone:

Pushing the boundaries of your comfort zone

Be honest – You might be living healthily and in accordance with your values in many ways, but chances are, deep down, you know that there are some things you should change, things which are adversely affecting your confidence levels. Be honest with yourself and allow yourself to acknowledge what these things are.

Focus your efforts – Zero in on the behaviour that you would like to change. For example, if you're stuck and tend to say no to new experiences because you're worried you won't be good enough, then make it part of your daily routine to list experiences you'd like to try, look out for opportunities coming your way and say yes more often. Being specific and deliberately focusing on saying yes is a lot more enabling than just deciding to try new things. Which new behaviours will benefit your confidence levels and how will you start to practise these?

Incentivise yourself – Make a list of all the good reasons to break an unhelpful habit and use this to incentivise yourself whenever you feel scared, insecure or like giving up. For instance, a better social life or greater achievements at work, which your current tendency to say no might be preventing. These would be real and very attractive benefits to feed your confidence – great incentives! What are your strongest and most compelling incentives?

Do something! – Set yourself up for success by taking immediate action. However small the first step, do it, and you'll find it leads to further actions as you build up momentum and your confidence grows.

Congratulate yourself – Take every opportunity to look out for nice and good things you are doing and make a point of acknowledging them. Say to yourself, 'What a kind thing to say' (rather than 'Ah, that was nothing'), 'Didn't I do well not giving up in those circumstances' (rather than 'How rubbish was I at that'), or 'I managed to fit in 30 minutes on the treadmill' (rather than 'I'm so rubbish, I should have done a 1 hour workout').

Enlist backup – Tell someone you trust what it is you intend to achieve. Not only can they help you recognise when you're slipping, but you're also much less likely to slip in the first place as you might lose face if you fail! Accountability can be key to staying on track or to recognising when you are straying from the path to success. Don't allow a fear of failure to prevent you from sharing your intentions! To whom will you tell your plans and intentions?

Accountability can be key to staying on track

Record your achievements – Keep careful notes of your progress and achievements and the benefits you are experiencing. Progress is a very effective incentive to keep going. Read more about keeping a success diary in "No one appreciates me".

Persevere – If you slip up, perhaps because you feel overly nervous, you're too hard on yourself or you let your insecurities stop you from doing something, don't be tempted to throw in the towel. Just get back on track and keep going. Failure is only a reality when you stop trying. See also "I'm an underachiever" for more on how to handle slips.

My fears are stupid!

In our efforts to overcome our fears and the hurdles they create for us, we often try to eliminate them entirely.

In doing so, we belittle our fears and beat ourselves up for having them, which doesn't do much good for our confidence levels.

The fact is that everyone has fears. They are normal, sometimes healthy and sometimes useful. In true fight or flight situations, they can save your life, as they often did for our ancestors on the savannah! However they are not healthy nor purposeful if you allow them to be blown out of proportion and to paralyse you. Being turned down for a date (or second date) or promotion really does not equal death. Being eaten by a lion does. Accept that all fears are not equal and act on them accordingly. Distinguish between your helpful and unhelpful fears. So allow yourself the chance of success with the date or your boss, but do not fight the lion!

But also be kind to yourself and accept the feelings of discomfort associated with certain situations. Those feelings aren't silly, but you don't have to allow them to dictate how you act or to paralyse you and prevent any action at all. See more about self-compassion and its benefits in "I was born negative".

Here are some questions you might like to ask yourself to overcome the impact of your fears:

Breaking the fear cycle

- What dreams have you never felt able to pursue?
- What would you love to achieve or experience that you've never found the courage or opportunity to try?
- What's the worst that could happen if you went for it? Be completely honest here! How dangerous are the potential consequences? Are they worth the risk? If they are, it's time to go for it. If they're genuinely not, it's time to let that dream go and find fulfilment elsewhere. And either way, enjoy the liberation!
- If you have decided that going for your dreams is worth the risk, see "I don't like change" for a strategy.

Knowledge

I don't have the skills

Do you lack confidence because you feel you're not qualified, knowledgeable or experienced enough?

Firstly, ask yourself, how important is that qualification, knowledge or experience? Do you need it, and why?

Perhaps it's not really that important, for example if it's not needed in your work or there are others in your life that can take responsibility for it. If so, then don't feel you need to hide your lack of skills or knowledge. Trying to be something you're not will feed your lack of confidence, albeit under a disguise of trying to appear and feel *more* confident. Give up this temptation and hold your head high.

If the answer is that you *do* need the said skill or ability, it might also be worth doing an audit of past performance – when have you performed well? There may be many examples when you consciously look for them (enlist a friend or a colleague here for a more objective view).

If you know you would benefit from improving or expanding your skills, invest some time into investigating how you can do this – do you need formal training, more experience or perhaps a mentor? Take responsibility for organising this.

Finally, if the thought of improving your skills or knowledge doesn't excite you perhaps you're not playing to your interests and natural abilities? You may need a change of direction, professionally or personally. Accept who you are and what you enjoy and take actions accordingly.

Most importantly, don't feel you need to hide your developmental needs. No one is good at everything, and we all have areas we can improve upon. Pretending to be something you're not is what's causing your lack of confidence.

See more on upskilling in "I'm not * enough", and if you're well-qualified but still feel like a fraud, see "I feel like a fraud".

Mind

My lack of confidence is justified

You probably feel, and even 'know', that you are good at certain things and rubbish at others. That certain things are possible or achievable whilst others are out of your reach or beyond your abilities.

Whatever your knowledge or beliefs around your own abilities and opportunities, you will filter everything that happens around you in accordance with these beliefs.

Let's briefly explore what I mean by filtering. We have a huge amount of stimuli coming at us all day every day, and we simply can't process everything – the sounds, smells, sights, physical sensations. Our senses help us by filtering out information, and they will choose what to take in and what to ignore, largely based on our preconceived ideas of how things are.

So if you 'know' that you're great at socialising and small talk, when you're at a party you will notice everyone who talks to you, who smiles at you and who nods when you speak. The ones that don't listen or drift away you may not notice at all, or you won't attach any importance to their acts. Or you may assume that they've been called away. You simply filter them out.

On the other hand if you 'know' that you're rubbish at something, or that something isn't possible for you, you'll filter information just as effectively to support this. So if your lack of confidence means you 'know' you're not good at small talk or at telling an

Events are actually completely neutral

entertaining story, the *only* person you're likely to notice in the room is the one who isn't listening. The smilers are only being polite or kind. Right?

But are they? Or could it be that they are actually enjoy listening to you? So could you be doing yourself, and them, a disservice?

Events are actually completely neutral. It's your own interpretation of them which determines your experience, and which dictates your level of confidence.

Here's something you can try to develop new, positive beliefs:

Developing confidence boosting beliefs

* Write a list of the things you feel you're lacking – your negative beliefs about yourself and your reality

- Identify the beliefs you'd most like to change

- Turn them on their heads by writing a list of things you'd like to believe to be true about yourself instead. What beliefs would really benefit you? What would you love to know to be true about yourself and your reality?

- Look for evidence of why you should already hold these beliefs. This may be challenging at first but have patience with yourself and look back – when in the past did your lack of confidence prevent you noticing evidence? For example, if your belief is that you always fail at interviews but you're currently in a job, that's an excellent example of you having succeeded at an interview. Another example could be to counteract a negative belief about your social life with examples of when you've enjoyed seeing friends or had a good conversation in the past month or two. Note down any examples you can think of. Perhaps also discuss this with a trusted friend who can help you find examples in your life

- Now think about how you can create more opportunities to replicate past, successful behaviours, to add more and more evidence to support your new positive beliefs

- You might want to use a success diary (see "No one appreciates me") to make sure you capture all of your evidence and record your progress. Practise, and allow yourself to get more and more familiar with your new self-beliefs

- You might also want to place your list of confidence boosting beliefs somewhere visible and read them daily – this is what coaches refer to as affirmations. It will keep them fresh in your mind and reinforce them at both conscious and subconscious levels

I feel like a fraud

Have you achieved things but simply can't enjoy them or take credit for them? Perhaps you're climbing the career ladder, you're raising a healthy and happy family or you have lots of friends and an active social life, yet you feel it's all been a fluke? Or you feel you're just doing what anyone in your situation would do so your efforts aren't special, or anything to feel proud or confident about?

You may be suffering from what is known as 'Imposter Syndrome'. Clinical psychologists P R Clance and S A Imes first came up with this term to describe 'high-achieving individuals marked by an inability to internalise their accomplishments and a persistent fear of being exposed as a "fraud"'.[3]

If this rings bells with you, you may say to yourself things like, 'You have no idea of what you're doing, it's only a matter of time until you're found out'.

What's actually likely to be true is that there are many examples in your life demonstrating your competence and abilities, however you're habitually dismissing or overlooking them.

Imposter Syndrome is a surprisingly common condition. In fact, it is believed that around 70%

Take comfort in knowing that you're not alone

of the world population suffers from such feelings at some point in their lives. So take comfort in knowing that you're not alone, and that this feeling is totally normal, although it doesn't mean it's true!

See "My lack of confidence is justified" for a method of how to start noticing and believing in your own abilities more.

---

3   Pauline R Clance, *The Imposter Phenomenon: Overcoming the Fear That Haunts Your Success, Peachtree, 1985*

I've just been lucky

Do you undervalue your own achievements because they, and the action you took to reach them, came easily to you?

Well, just because something feels easy for you (for instance numbers, empathy, sport) it doesn't mean it's not special or not something to feel proud of and confident about. To someone else these things might be very difficult, just like the things you find difficult might come easily to them.

Also, when someone compliments you, don't shrug it off! Enjoy the praise, accept the compliment and allow yourself to acknowledge that it's down to your *abilities*.

Also see how the use of a success diary can help in "No one appreciates me".

I try to be positive but I can't

It's possible that in your efforts to think positively about yourself you actually find yourself doing the exact opposite.

When people try to make themselves feel better and more positive there is a tendency to use phrases such as, 'Don't stress', 'Don't worry', 'Don't be silly', but there is a problem with these statements because we humans can't process a negative! So when you say these things to yourself, you are thinking about the very things you don't want to think about in an effort to clear them from your mind, resulting in you focusing on what you're trying to eliminate, and reinforcing your lack of confidence.

How about trying, 'I'll be fine', 'I'm great', or 'I can handle this' instead?

Give one or both of the following ideas a try to shift your focus to the positive:

Improving your positive focus

* Ask people close to you what negative language they hear you use. Ask them to listen out for it and tell you whenever you use a negative expression

* Ask the same people to use positive expressions when speaking to you. If your partner, parent, best friend or others use expressions such as, 'Don't worry', think of an alternative that would be more effective such as, 'You'll be great' and ask them to use this instead

This might need a bit of practice!

See also 'I was born negative' for more on positive thinking techniques.

I'm not * enough

* Fill in your own blank!

Do you believe you'd be more confident if only you were more 'something'? Perhaps more outgoing, successful, intelligent, optimistic, popular?

But do you know what being more of that 'something' would look like exactly?

It's important to be specific about what your 'something' means to you if you want to have more of it. Knowing what you are aiming at will then allow you to explore whether you need training, experience, a formal qualification or maybe just some new habits and beliefs. Examples might be to have greater assertiveness skills, gain chartered status within your field of work or to be more mindful of how you make a difference.

When it comes to formal qualifications make sure you do your research – which qualification would give you the status, integrity, confidence and/or know-how you need? Which course would take you to the next level in your field of work, which parenting class would give you the insights you need, or which public speaking trainer would suit your needs?

If it's formal skills you need, remember that they're not personal or innate – we can all educate ourselves so do not be tempted to think that others are better than you because they have knowledge which you do not – they are simply educated in ways you are not, and you have the freedom to go and get yourself educated too.

When it comes to more personal attributes it can be useful to look for a role model who already possesses and acts upon the attributes you feel would give you the confidence you seek. This might sound a little odd, however the fact is that from birth we all learn how to behave, what's socially acceptable, what's funny, naughty, dangerous, good manners and so on from the people around us. If your parents stopped at red lights, said thank you and offered their seats for the elderly, the chances are you do too.

You have the freedom to go and get yourself educated

This kind of modelling is powerful and as an adult, you can use it to your advantage in a more deliberate sense. Here's how:

Mimicking a role model

Think of a person who already exudes the confidence you desire.

Watch them and note *specific* details of their:
- posture
- facial expressions
- tone of voice
- gestures
- style of dress
- interactions with others
- anything else that contributes to their air of confidence

Model yourself on this person and mimic them. Start when you're in the company of people that you're comfortable with, and as you get more familiar with your new behaviour, try it out in different and less familiar situations

Take notice of:
- what it feels like
- how others react to you
- how others look at you
- how others talk to you

This may feel a little strange at first, but remember that no one else knows you're 'mimicking' and it's no different to what you did as a child. Pick and choose what works for you and feel your confidence grow.

I get easily overwhelmed

Does your level of confidence waver when feeling overwhelmed? Do you often feel like too many things are coming at you from too many different angles, and that you don't know how to cope?

You may think that to be a confident person you must be confident in all situations and across all areas of life. But this kind of thinking is likely to result in you spreading yourself too thinly and therefore achieving very little. Or at the very least leave you with the *feeling* that you're achieving little. And how you feel about it is all that matters to your confidence.

Confidence is situation specific

It might help to know that confidence is situation specific. For instance, delivering a presentation with confidence is very different to feeling confident about sitting an exam. By extension then, even if you feel insecure in one setting, it doesn't mean you won't feel confident in others, but by generalising, you're failing to acknowledge the confident times and encouraging the feelings of being overwhelmed.

At times when you're most struggling with confidence, it might help to learn to laugh. The psychological benefits of laughter are incredibly helpful to anyone who is vulnerable to feeling overwhelmed. When you laugh, you allow yourself to gain perspective, reducing the 'swamped' feeling and strengthening your resilience by creating a psychological distance between you and the situation you're in. This will enable you to see more choices, feel less threatened and establish a more realistic point of view.

So the next time you feel overwhelmed, try considering the options you have available and give yourself an opportunity to relax by laughing rather than complaining or focusing on the negatives – this will help you to handle the situation in a better way and boost your confidence as a result.

I'm an underachiever

Do you go about life feeling like you have achieved very little? Does your lack of confidence hold you back? Are your insecurities getting in the way of you achieving what you desire? Maybe they stop you progressing at work, meeting the right partner or enjoying a fulfilling social life?

It's important to be aware of the fact that the past does not equal the future and it's never too late to start achieving. There are plenty of famous examples of this, such as the actor Morgan Freeman, who was 50 years old when he had his breakthrough role in the film 'Street Smart'. This was also the magic number for Charles Darwin, whose book 'On the Origin of the Species' was published when he turned 50. Even later success was achieved by the eventual multi-millionaire Darrell Hammond, who founded KFC when he was 62 years of age.

In the field of coaching we often ask, 'If you don't know where you're going, how will you know when you get there?' Having clarity on your destination and setting a goal for yourself is the most effective first step to achievement. A goal provides you with purpose and direction, gives you clarity on what you need to be doing, feeling and experiencing and enables you to make a detailed plan. The goal is a guide which will widen your horizon and encourage you to go for things much bigger and better than what you have now. Without this, you are effectively walking in the wild, with no clarity on the destination you'd like to reach. The chances of actually ending up anywhere near where you'd like to are therefore pretty slim.

Setting goals

Here's how you can start setting goals and taking steps toward achieving them:

Think of something you've always wanted to achieve. It doesn't have to be something big, such as travelling the world or changing careers; if you'd rather start small how about visiting a relative abroad or learning a new skill?

Now let's make that goal effective – first, let's make it a **SMART** one:

Specific – If you're not specific about what you want to have, feel and do it will be difficult for you to get there. You might get lucky, but the chances are you won't.

Measurable – You need to be able to measure your progress and you need to know what needs to happen for a goal to be achieved. I'll cover this in more detail later.

Achievable – Consider whether the achievement of your goal hinges on certain practicalities. Does it require an investment in time or money, or do you need to be in a certain place? Don't set yourself up to fail if there are things outside of your control. However this is a balancing act as we are often capable of achieving a lot more than we believe or give ourselves credit for. Perhaps part of the plan could be freeing up time or finances by giving something up?

Realistic – Be careful not to expect too much too soon. This would only knock your confidence further. However, once more, be a little careful of paying too much attention to this rule, for the same reasons as for Achievable above. I bet you can achieve far more than you think is realistic!

Timely – Give yourself a deadline – if you don't you could find yourself discussing, analysing and dreaming about the same goal in a year or more's time! I often recommend timescales that are around 6 months in length, as that's enough time to achieve some real changes, but not so far off that there's a lack of a sense of urgency.

SMART should have helped you clarify the goal. Now let's turn to the person who's going to achieve it – *you!*

RACE will help with this:

Responsibility – Unless you take full responsibility for reaching your goal, you will never attain it. That ownership is vital! We often blame others or our circumstances for our own failings or insecurities but only we can take the action needed to reach our goals.

Action – Often we plan, discuss and make decisions about what we'll do and how we'll improve things, and whilst doing so we feel like we are moving closer to our goals. But thinking is not doing! It's only when you actually take action and *do* something that you start making progress. Collectively, small steps will add up to big progress so focus on taking at least one small action in the right direction every day.

Commitment – You'll need to be committed! Ultimately, implementing change in your life will involve taking yourself out of your comfort zone (see more in "I don't like change") and when the going gets tough you'll need to be 100% committed to yourself and your own development.

Emotion – If you aren't emotionally attached to your goal, you'll soon lose sight of it. So it's important that the goal comes from *you* – if it is set for the benefit of someone else, for example to please your partner or parent, you won't be emotionally connected to it.

Write your goal down. Make sure you use positive language, focusing on what you *do* want rather than what you *don't* want. See more about the importance of using positive language in "I try to be positive but I can't".

I also strongly recommend you write your goal in first person and present tense – as if you're already living and enjoying it. Then place it somewhere visible (but private if you prefer) and read it every day. This is powerful because your subconscious does not know the difference between fiction and reality[4] and by reading your goal daily, and in first person and present tense, your subconscious will begin to believe it is true, which makes it a lot more likely that you'll make it happen.

Now you may be wondering *how* you'll achieve all of this – how you'll move from where you are now to the end goal. I recommend you allow yourself to ignore the *hows* and instead focus on the *whats*. What you need to decide, join, commit to, organise, borrow, learn, feel, talk about, look like, behave like and so on in order to progress.

So make a plan – a clear path of all the major steps in chronological order with timescales, from today to

4   *Sandy MacGregor, CALM – Subconscious mind does not know the difference https://www.youtube.com/watch?v=jzlxlx87c7k*

your deadline. By setting out what you need to do, you'll be in a position to figure out how you'll implement the steps later. It's hard to answer how until you know what needs to be done.

The more specific you are in what the steps towards your goal look like the better. For example, rather than stating that 'by the 15th June, I'll be making a positive impact at work', phrase it in a more specific way: 'by the 15th June, I will be sharing my knowledge at every opportunity at work by contributing at meetings, circulating relevant articles and providing timely feedback to team members'. Even better, you might like to split such a step into three separate ones, increasing your focus and ability to achieve them further.

Also, make sure you focus the steps on what *you* will do rather than what others need to do, say or change. So rather than stating that your boss will appreciate you more or that your partner will give you regular cuddles, think of steps you could take to increase the likelihood of these things happening. Don't set yourself up to fail by giving away the power to other people or circumstances. Keep the locus of control!

Keep the locus of control!

See also "No one appreciates me" for more on how to recognise your own achievements.

I can't maintain things

Do you find yourself feeling good and on top of things one minute and then not so good the next? Do you feel like there's no point in trying, that you're never going to get anywhere anyway?

This probably leads to the perception that the only possible outcome is further failures, along with a further decline in your confidence.

The good news is that not only is a different, more positive, successful and confident future possible, but the bumpy road you're experiencing is perfectly normal! So you're not alone, nor are you 'a failure'.

When we work towards something, or implement some kind of change in our lives, we need to be clear on the outcome, clear on the steps (see more in "I'm an underachiever") and take regular action but we also need to allow for some slippage along the way. If you are vulnerable to feelings of failure, you may be making the common mistake of expecting the road to success to be straight but this is rarely the reality, not even for the most successful and confident of people.

So you're enjoying your own progress and enjoying the resulting growth in confidence. Then suddenly, *wham*, you hit an obstacle, and you're thrown off course.

The good news is that this sort of regression is not personal. It's a natural and normal part of the growth process. And it often happens when we least expect it to. Possibly because the progress was starting to feel a little easier and you took your eye off the ball, so old habits kicked back in and you're back to where you started (see "I can't cope with criticism" for more about autopilot behaviour). Or it may be that an unexpected challenge came along to derail you.

It's perfectly natural and perhaps even predictable that this may happen, so don't beat yourself up as this will only lead to further regression. The thing to do is to *keep going*. You may not feel confident at this point, but pressing on is the only way to get back on track.

> Pressing on is the only way to get back on track

I'd hate to become arrogant

There's a common misconception that being confident means being cocky or a 'know it all'. The reality is that arrogant, self-important or cocky individuals may well be hiding their own insecurities or fragile egos.

In fact, truly confident individuals don't need to show off their abilities or shout their opinions to the world, as they are comfortable in their own skin and don't need the approval, agreement or recognition of others. It's certainly true that you can choose to be confident *and* keep all the other qualities you feel are important.

Knowing your own mind and feeling confident in your abilities, opinions and decisions doesn't mean you necessarily disagree, disrespect or dislike someone else's choices or efforts. Being kind, modest and generous are completely compatible with a confident style, as you have nothing to prove. This allows you to focus outwardly on those around you rather than inwardly on your own needs and thoughts, freeing you up to display positive behaviours with a peaceful mind. The arrogant person has the opposite focus – it's all about them!

Truly confident individuals don't need to show off their abilities

I have too many regrets

When you evaluate your past decisions and actions do you do so from a critical and judgmental point of view? This can act as a barrier to future decision making and positive actions.

This happens when your lack of confidence in yourself and your own decision making result in you looking for guarantees that you'll make the 100% right decision, and that it'll result in the perfect outcome.

This is of course impossible, often resulting in paralysis and an inability to make decisions and progress them positively. Or rather, in effect, decisions actually being made to stay right where you are. Which then drains your confidence further.

A vicious, confidence draining cycle is then born (see 'I'm scared of failure' for more).

So rather than giving into this, remember that the past does not equal the future, and allow yourself to be freed from the paralysis you're experiencing. Because the future is the unknown, and you can only make decisions and act in accordance with the information available to you in the *present.*

Also, when you find yourself judging your past decisions, try reminding yourself that memory is never a reliable source. It's inherently flawed and changes over time. So you cannot have clarity on all the considerations and factors which were present at the time of making a decision when looking back. Therefore, judging yourself retrospectively will never be a fair game. Once you accept this and give up the judging, you'll be more forgiving and kinder to yourself which reduces the pressure that you put yourself under to guarantee a perfect outcome.

In turn, your confidence will grow and, instead of being stuck in the past, you'll be liberated to move forward positively. See "I was born negative" for more on self-compassion.

It's worth considering that there will of course be times when you've made mistakes. Perhaps even mistakes that could have been avoided. The truth is that this happens to *everyone*, and it is in fact the way we learn and develop as humans. It provides you with feedback on how *not* to do something and, if accepted as simply that, allows you to look for new and better options to try out. See it as valuable information and use it to empower rather than paralyse you and your future progress. See "No one appreciates me" for more on feedback.

I was born negative

Some people adopt a negative or glass-half-empty kind of outlook because it prevents disappointment and means they won't appear naïve or overly confident or big-headed (see also "I'd hate to become arrogant").

But if this sounds like you, does it actually make you feel good to constantly put yourself, your opportunities or your achievements down?

In our heads, we talk to ourselves all the time, but are you listening to what you're saying? Is the glass-half-empty attitude making you focus only on negatives?

I often say be careful what you say to yourself, because you'll be listening! And your thoughts largely determine your feelings. So if you want to feel more confident deprecating thoughts won't do you much good. And if you repeat something often enough, you'll start believing it. Feeding a vicious cycle of negative chatter and resulting in negative feelings.

Be careful
what you say
to yourself,
because you'll
be listening!

Importantly, your thoughts determine not only how you feel, but also the likely outcome of your actions. So your success, happiness and resulting confidence levels really are intrinsically linked to your thoughts!

So, if you tend to think negatively, and to focus on what's missing from your life, you really are running the risk of preventing success and joy, or failing to appreciate it.

How you respond to events is what shapes your experiences, *not* the events themselves. Taking responsibility for your own view of the world and your responses to the events in it will allow you much greater control over outcomes than you may currently realise you have.

One of the most effective ways to feel better and gain or maintain a positive mindset is to combat the negative mind chatter and develop a habit of looking at things from a positive point of view.

I'm sure this is not the first time you've heard about the importance of positive thinking and of course, if it was easy, we'd all be doing it all the time! So here are a few ideas on how you can make your thoughts more positive, ensuring they serve you rather than hinder you:

Positive self-talk techniques

The first thing to realise is that you *are* in control. Many people feel like they are at the complete mercy of their own self-talk. Like it's being said *to* them rather than *by* them. So accept that you own your own thoughts – they do not own you! Once you accept and claim that responsibility, if your thoughts aren't supporting and aiding you, you can practice new ones. Importantly though, this point is about developing positive thinking habits, rather than trying to shut up the negative ones entirely. The latter would actually put the emphasis on the negativity, and would also likely result in you giving yourself a hard time for 'failing' to shut them up

Accept that thoughts are just thoughts, *not* reality or the truth. You can think the thought that lions are green but that doesn't make lions green! You wouldn't believe your own thoughts in this example, so be careful not to confuse other thoughts with truth

- Don't let negative self-talk become part of you. When you do, it has an enormous hold over your feelings and your self-confidence. An effective trick here is to acknowledge negative thoughts when they show up and talk about them to yourself. Maybe something along the lines of, 'Aha, here's my "I'm an idiot" thought', or, "Hello there "I'm incompetent" thoughts, I know you well'. You'll find this will reduce the thoughts' hold over you and reduce their importance, allowing you to see them for what they are – just words! Over time, you can acknowledge them more quickly, allowing them to exist without fighting with them or allowing them to become part of who you are

- My fourth tip is to be more aware of when you're indulging in overly dramatic speculation. What does that mean? Well, we humans don't cope very well with ambiguity. So if something happens (e.g. you say hello to someone), then there is a gap (you're waiting for their response) and then there is an unexpected outcome (they don't say hello back), you probably fill in the gap in the middle and make up your own stories. In this scenario, you might then start thinking of all the reasons why the person ignored you – how they must dislike you, or how you must have done something to upset them, what a terrible person you must be, and so on. In this example, you can see how dramatic the thinking became really rather quickly, resulting in a spiral of negativity. But the person may just have not heard you. Maybe their own self-talk was in overdrive so your 'hello' didn't even register! Whatever the reason, there's no point in speculating, and you convincing yourself that you're somehow responsible or at fault is obviously not helpful. Not only does it make you feel bad but you're most likely wrong anyhow. The fact is that you really don't know! Human nature means we're busy with our own reality. You can pretty safely assume it's rarely about you and all about the other person

- Actively look for the positives in situations and seek out the things for which you are grateful. Even in dire circumstances there is always a silver lining and when you identify and appreciate this, you'll boost your mood and general wellbeing. The power of this was beautifully demonstrated by a client of mine who fell seriously ill and rather than focusing on her pains and fears, she chose to feel thankful and comforted by the warmth and care that she received from those she held dear. The positive impact of gratitude is well researched and a popular method to implement more of it in your life is to start a gratitude journal. Simply note down what you are grateful for at the end of every day and enjoy the positive emotions of greater happiness and peace of mind that follow[5]

• Now let's look at the Rubbish Bin strategy which a client of mine developed. She is a talented and intelligent woman, yet she struggled with low levels of confidence and particularly suffered from self-doubt when entering meetings with very senior people at work. To tackle her negative mind chatter she visualised herself, in her mind's eye, scrunching up her negative thoughts and chucking them in the rubbish bin before entering such meetings. This way she allowed herself to clear her mind of the clutter and became more focused, more confident and more able to hear and follow what everyone else were saying in the room

• Or you could try the Happy Song strategy. Another client of mine developed this. He identified a song from his youth that reminds him of happy times and

---

5   *Read more about gratitude in Thanks! How Practicing Gratitude Can Make You Happier by Robert Emmons, Mariner Books, 2008*

which gives him a sense of joy and calm. By saving it on his phone, he's now able to play it whenever he starts to notice his self-talk veering towards worry and self-doubt

* Another client when she had a lovely holiday in Cornwall one summer brought home a pebble. She now carries the pebble in her pocket when she's doing something important or daunting, and she simply touches or holds it whenever the occasion calls for it, allowing her to remain calm and confident. This we call the Calming Anchor technique

You may now be able to think of your own personal strategy, which will help you to stay positive and to feel centred, in control and confident. You can do it!

Be aware that your body doesn't differentiate between criticism received by others and the criticism you create yourself, and it responds to both in the same way by triggering the stress hormones cortisone and adrenaline. Self-compassion is a concept that is gaining momentum at the moment. It helps to release the calming hormone oxytocin and endorphins which enable your body and mind to relax. To practise self-compassion, try to accept that the inner critic is nothing more than a bully and reduce the attention you pay it (see points 2 and 3 above). Also accept that the inner critic has likely to have been with you since childhood (children often protect themselves from others' criticism by trying to 'beat them to it') so it'll take practice to change the habit – only with self-compassion can you allow this learning curve, avoiding the common pitfall of giving yourself a hard time for the fact that you're giving yourself a hard time! Forgive yourself for not being perfect – perfection is unattainable and imperfection is a fundamental part of being human. And if your inner bully doesn't listen straight away, forgive it too![6]

When you've chosen a positive thinking technique from the list above, here's how to implement it:

Developing a more positive disposition

- Look out for times when negative self-talk is kicking in. Listen to yourself and start to recognise the signs of it happening

- Deliberately apply the positive self-talk technique of your choice to interrupt the negative chatter. Have patience here – it's a brand new behaviour and practice will be needed before it becomes comfortable and eventually habitual

6   Read more on self-compassion in *The Mindful Path to Self-Compassion: Freeing Yourself from Destructive Thoughts and Emotions* by Christopher K Gerber, Guilford Press, 2009, and on Kristin Neff's website *http://self-compassion.org*

- After consistently applying the technique for a month, review how well it's working. If you recognise some progress, keep at it, but if you feel it's not effective try out a different technique

- After another month, review again and continue the technique if it's working. You may wish to try an additional one now too, to work in conjunction with each other

Once you're thinking more positively, notice how your confidence increases.

You might also want to read about how to use a smile to your advantage in "I'm an introvert".

I'm a perfectionist

Calling oneself a perfectionist can be rather attractive. After all, it implies we do things perfectly!

However, it can be disabling and can result in you feeling like you never reach the right standard or that you never reach the finishing line. If you're constantly trying to perfect something before pressing 'send' or handing it over, you're achieving very little and probably feel dissatisfied about the things you do complete. This habit could be hiding a lack of confidence under the disguise of doing things really well.

Does the attraction of being a perfectionist still seem so attractive? If you instead think of it in terms of, 'I'm so insecure about my own performance that I obsess and tinker for ages before I even dare show anyone what I'm doing', you might appreciate that it's not a helpful mindset.

> Because you get more of what you focus on!

We often ask ourselves questions, and if you ask questions you will give yourself answers. So if you're asking, 'How is this lacking?' or 'What have I not done well enough?' you will find the answers, zooming in on the ways in which you or your performance is lacking, even if it's close to perfect. Because you get more of what you focus on!

So instead try asking yourself, 'How is this piece great?', 'What have I done really well?' or 'What do I bring to this situation?' You will find positive answers and feel better about yourself because of them.

Perfectionists also have a tendency to use absolutes in language such as 'always', 'never', 'must' and so on. This kind of all-or-nothing thinking results in a perception that if things are not perfect they are failures, leaving your confidence levels vulnerable.

Here are two examples:

I always have to win

So you cannot enjoy your 9 out of 10 wins because you lost once? This suggests a 90% success rate is valueless, which seems harsh, I'm sure you'll agree. How about 'I have an excellent track record of winning'? Much more accurate, and much more likely to make you feel good about yourself.

To be good at my job I must never miss a deadline

On the face of it this may seem like a good attitude to have. However, whilst the intention is to be professional and conscientious, that 'never' puts you under an unreasonable amount of pressure. How about 'I'm good at my job and I'm great at meeting deadlines'? Again, more accurate and more helpful to your confidence levels.

Finally, do you believe that 'practice makes perfect'? Actually, practice doesn't make perfect. Perfection is an unattainable goal. So as long as perfection is your measure of success, you're setting yourself up to fail and by doing so, you damage your confidence. The better you know something the more confident you'll feel, because actually, practice makes *confidence*.

I'm an introvert

There is a common myth in today's world that to be confident you must be outgoing and extroverted. A gregarious, charismatic personality type has been popularised and admired throughout the Western World and media for many years.

But the truth is that actually an introvert can be just as, if not more, confident.

Introversion, or a more quiet, contemplative style is not inferior to extroversion, or a sign of lacking in confidence.

So instead of trying to adopt a fake, loud or overly chatty disposition which isn't really 'you', learn to interact with others in whatever way you feel comfortable.

If you don't know how to do this, try a smile! A smile with eye contact can exude just as much confidence to those around you as a loud voice. And in turn you'll feed your own feelings of confidence.

Smile, whether you feel like it or not

I often say, 'Smile, whether you feel like it or not. And particularly when you don't!' The reason being that it's pretty hard to feel insecure or negative while smiling. Even when you're forced to smile (for example by putting a pen between your teeth) it makes you feel happier. This happens because when you're smiling you activate the zygomatic muscle in your cheek, which signals to your brain that you're happy. Which in turn encourages you to smile even more!

So your smiles boost your mood and reduce your feelings of stress and insecurity. This leaves you better able to make confident decisions and take positive, determined actions, which in turn reduces the initial source of the stress, enabling an ongoing positive cycle.

Testing the positive power of your smile

Try this – deliberately smile. Now try to think of something negative without losing the smile. It's hard! When we smile it sends a message to our brain that life is good. Now focus on what's good about you and your life and notice your confidence growing.

And when you're ready, try out that smile at meetings, appointments and social events – anywhere where you'd usually feel uncomfortable because other people are more outgoing than you. Notice how people react, and if they respond more positively, how that makes you feel.[7]

---

7   Read more about this in articles by Natasha Mann at http://www.netdoctor.co.uk/healthy-living/benefits-of-smiling.htm and Harold E Sconier at http://www.livestrong.com/article/18859-health-benefits-smiling/

I was born with poor confidence

It's a common misconception that you're either born confident or you're not, and that it's part of your nature. But thankfully this is not true and confidence is actually a skill, just like many others, which can be learnt.

If you believe you're not confident you may be subconsciously adopting negative or unconfident body language. People make up their minds about each other in two ways – by what they say, and by how they say it. And here's where it gets interesting: only 20% of the judgments people make about you are based on what you say. The other 80% are based on how you say it. So whether you're perceived as a confident or unconfident person is largely determined by non-verbal cues like your posture, tone of voice and facial expression.

> Those who walk around with their heads held high not only get the respect of others, they also seem to respect themselves

And perhaps more importantly, your body language also determines how you think and feel about *yourself*. In 2011 the Economist published an article about this – how our body language not only determines the impression we make on others, but how it also influences our feelings about ourselves. The article suggested that a person's posture may affect their self-esteem more than, say, being assigned management responsibilities. It said that, 'those who walk around with their heads held high not only get the respect of others, they also seem to respect themselves'.[8]

In short, your body language determines whether you feel confident or not. Of course, you are able to change your body language, and the more you practise positive body language the easier and more natural it will feel.

What's more, displaying powerful and confident body language (chest out, arms in a winner's pose, etc) before entering a challenging situation has been found to result in more positive results. In one experiment participants were tested in a stressful job interview situation. Some did high power poses before the interview and some did low power ones. Guess who got the job? Yes, those who'd done the high power ones! The confident power poses were deliberately adopted before the interview so they were not visible to the interviewers, but they clearly changed something in the interviewees.

The message here is that you have much greater power over how you feel and appear to others than

8   http://www.economist.com/node/17899714

you may think! You can choose what body language you display. So smile, hold your head high and the confidence will follow.[9]

In conclusion, rather than labelling yourself as inherently lacking in confidence or beating yourself up over your perceived shortcomings, accept that confidence is a skill. Just like driving a car or playing a game, it can be learnt. Indeed, just like a muscle, it can be strengthened with practice and repetition.

> Hold your head high and the confidence will follow

If there are situations in which you do feel confident (family gatherings for instance), how do you behave then? What body language do you use, what tone or speed of speaking? Start to practise this behaviour in situations where you feel less confident.

Also see how you can mimic a role model in "I'm not * enough". This may be particularly helpful if you struggle to think of situations in your own life that you can build upon.

---

9   *See more about this in a TED talk by Dr Amy Cuddy at http://www.ted.com/talks/amy_cuddy_your_body_language_shapes_who_you_are*

Other people

I can't cope with criticism

Do you frequently find yourself feeling offended and under fire? Do you find that you often adopt a self-defensive stance to protect yourself from upset or possible criticism? Does this self-protection typically leave you feeling more secure and confident? I'm guessing not, as these are destructive thoughts and feelings, created as a result of your perception that the world is critical of you and forcing you to defend yourself. Does this sound familiar?

The fact is that for the majority of the time we all operate on autopilot, meaning that you act, react, make decisions and think in accordance with your habits. So this perception of others being critical of you and the resulting self-defensive response are both likely to be habits you've developed over time. It may be that an important role model early on in your life demonstrated these strong reactions in the face of feedback or criticism, teaching you that this is the right way to respond. Alternatively, it may have been true that someone was overly critical of you at some point in the past, but that doesn't mean it's necessarily true now, nor that it's true of all people. It's just that your taught behaviour is to react, think and experience others' behaviour and comments in line with your expectations of criticism, leaving your confidence and self-worth damaged, and you repeatedly feeling hurt and vulnerable.

Let's look at why we develop these kinds of autopilot responses or habits. It is estimated that our autopilot drives 90% of our daily behaviour. When you engage in habits you do so without consciously thinking about what you are doing, leaving your brainpower available for other tasks. Repeated behaviour forms neurological pathways which are shortcuts in your brain for efficiently processing routine tasks.

Here's an example: if you're a driver, you'll remember how when you were learning to drive each action was carefully considered and deliberate and now you do those things without thinking. The pattern of 'mirror, signal, manoeuvre' is now a habit, with a strong neurological pathway attached to it, leaving you free to think about the meeting you're driving to, the scenery outside or the song on the radio. When you were concentrating on processing each task involved with this relatively complex action, you most likely filtered out all of these things, but now that a neurological pathway is in place, you have freed up the capacity to appreciate them.

If you frequently feel like you're under fire, you may have developed an autopilot response of feeling attacked, criticised or somehow threatened and you may then become defensive, lash out or perhaps withdraw from the situation.

Whilst your autopilot is often useful in saving you time and energy because you don't have to relearn what you're doing

You do have a choice in how you respond to others

every time you do it, when it causes you to automatically feel challenged and criticised this isn't likely to boost your confidence and you need to retrain it.[10]

The good news is that you do have a choice in how you respond to others and you can decide to develop new responses and more helpful habits.

Ask yourself, how would I respond if someone's comment, opinion or feedback genuinely wasn't critical of me? If they were simply expressing a different opinion or toying with ideas, without a critical agenda?

Instead of shutting down and feeling offended, angry or hurt, what would it be like to listen, consider their point of view and even try out some of their ways of thinking or operating?

The fact is people will always have different opinions and perspectives on things. It isn't personal. It happens to everyone!

---

10   *Read more about this in an article by Julie Poland at http://thesummitblog.blogspot.se/2010/07/overcoming-inner.html*

And isn't that how we develop and learn, through discussion with others? But you can only do that when you stop treating their opinions as criticisms of you and allow yourself to hear and consider their different point of view.

Of course, it may be that there are people in your life who are indeed overly critical or judgmental. However it's your choice as to how you respond to these people and how you allow them to influence you. A defensive stance will only feed your negative emotions, whilst accepting their viewpoint calmly will not only leave your confidence intact, but also encourage them to hear your own views more clearly. Or frustrate them enough to stop the criticisms and judgements!

If the above resonates with you, try working through the following questions:

Developing greater resilience to criticism

- Where in your life do you often end up feeling frustrated, annoyed or insecure? Who are the main 'offenders'?

- How would it feel to accept their viewpoint whilst still feeling strong in your own decisions or actions? To listen to others' perspectives whilst not allowing them to challenge your own unnecessarily? Note down how you'd think and act when taking this calmer and more self-assured approach

* How could your typical behaviour or responses in these situations be contributing to your negative experience? Be honest with yourself and consider options without trying to predict how the other person might respond. Give them, and yourself, a chance

This exercise is not about taking responsibility for the other person but merely for yourself. They may still have flaws and, for you, annoying or inappropriate views or habits. This is about you finding out how you can encourage a more positive or better functioning relationship in order to boost your confidence in the relevant situation.

If, however, you still feel certain that some people in your life are too critical, negative or judgmental it may be that you should consider doing a social audit! Because some people can, and do, have a big negative influence on the confidence of those around them.

Here are three ways in which this type of person could be affecting your confidence:

Making you feel guilty – Negative and judgmental people often make others feel obscurely guilty, as if they are somehow responsible and to blame for their own problems. If this is happening in your life, you probably find yourself walking on eggshells to make sure that you don't say or do anything that will upset the person further, and every tiptoeing step will drain your confidence further.

Dominating – Negative and judgmental people can exert power over those around them causing them to have to be overly careful before they act or speak. They dominate and dictate unhealthily within their relationships, and if this is happening to you it will leave your confidence drained.

Making you doubt yourself – Being negative, cynical and miserable about life in general can give the impression of being knowledgeable and intelligent, or of having superior and profound philosophical knowledge that others (happy, 'shallow' people) can't possibly appreciate. If you have someone like this in your life, you may soon find yourself doubting your own intelligence and worth.

Do any of these scenarios exist in your life? Then it may be time to consider whether you need certain people in your life if they do nothing but drain your confidence.

No one appreciates me

If you're feeling under-appreciated and this is destroying your self-confidence, you may be relying too much on what other people think of you.

When you rely heavily on other people to feel good about yourself or to know that something you've completed is good or that you've made a good decision, you may be relying too heavily on what's known as an external feedback system. While this is quite common, it can be debilitating. If you always need someone else's approval your self-esteem is likely to be pretty low.

> You may be relying too heavily on what's known as an external feedback system

This is of course bad news for your ability to enjoy and build on your own successes. Many achievements will be missed, either because no one was there to tell you how well you'd done so you didn't celebrate them, or because you doubted yourself too much to give yourself a chance in the first place. A big 'lose-lose', I'm sure you will agree!

Also, if you have this predominantly external focus, you may blame how you feel about your life and experiences on external circumstances: the people and events that exist and happen around you. That happen *to* you.

However, if this resonates with you, you are likely to be selling yourself short. Because you have more control than that. You can *choose* your reactions to the events around you.

The opposite of an external focus is an internal feedback system. That's when you know you're worth it, good enough and competent, right, able, strong, self-sufficient and so on, without the need for someone else to tell you. Imagine how much more in control of your feelings, your achievements and indeed yourself and your self-confidence you will be when you subscribe to this system.

Let's look at one of the most famous and revered men in the world who heavily relied on a strong, confident internal feedback system – Nelson Mandela.

Mr Mandela studied law on and off for 50 years. He failed about half the courses he took.

He started his studies in 1939 and persevered to finally secure a law degree while in prison in 1989.

Imagine if he had needed external verification that he was doing the right thing! Thankfully he didn't look for this verification, either for his law studies or in pursuit of his other convictions.

Some days things will feel tough, you'll doubt yourself and wonder if it's really worth the effort. This is when self-recognition is vital! Here's a suggestion on how you can give yourself the positive feedback you need.

Keeping a daily success diary

Note down your successes at the end of every day – what went well? Quick and easy bullet points will do. This will help you to focus on the things you did well and to take a pride in your successes. This list of successes will grow both on the page and in your memory bank. What you focus on you get more of, and on days when you need some positive feedback to feel better about yourself you have a confidence boosting record to look back on too.

I've been hurt in the past

Has someone left your confidence in tatters? Perhaps they made comments or acted in ways that you struggle to understand or forgive?

There is a common myth about confidence that once it's lost, it can never again be regained. If you believe this you may be making it your reality.

Thankfully it is untrue. It does take guts to start building your confidence back up after it's been damaged, but once you're there you'll be much more resilient than you were before and less likely to have your confidence shaken again.

There are absolutely times when it's quite healthy, and you are quite right to allow yourself, to feel hurt, sad or angry – when these emotions are part of dealing with difficult events and of coming to terms with them.

The problems arise when you continue to dwell on what has happened for a disproportionate amount of time. Thinking back, you may recognise this has happened in the past – when you continue to talk about something months, or even years, after it happened. You may recognise this in friends if not yourself, as we often find it easier to see things in those around us than in ourselves. This kind of dwelling on the past can be as hurtful as the original act and consequently damaging to your confidence and general wellbeing.

Two harmful drivers are at play in these situations.

Firstly, memory is inherently unreliable, resulting in the possibility that some of the factors that you feel absolutely convinced happened or were present at the time of the hurtful act may actually not have existed, or at least not in the way you remember them. Every time we retell something we unwittingly alter the story slightly and as the probability of memory being flawed

> Every time you retell a story, in your mind or to someone else, you relive it, damaging your confidence further

increases with time you can be pretty certain you won't remember things exactly how they happened a long time after the event. This is not about you being un-justified in feeling angry or hurt, but about your painful feelings being enhanced and negatively strengthened by flawed memories.

Secondly, you give away control over how you are feeling when you dwell on past hurts. You allow the person who hurt you to continue to do so over and over again. Every time you retell a story, in your mind or to someone else, you relive it, damaging your confidence further. In doing this you are giving away the power over how you are feeling. The thing is, whilst someone may have done something unjust to you in the past, you alone are responsible for protracting the hurt by ruminating and continually going over the event in your mind. By doing so, they are still in control, but they nev-er asked for it. And certainly they do not deserve it. Ac-cept that this is your choice and you can choose to stop.

This doesn't mean you need to condone what was done to you. Nor does it mean that person (or situation) is welcome back into your life. It's instead about you moving on, leaving them and, more importantly, their acts in the past.

Of course this requires courage – both to actively let go of an upset, even if there is every justification to hold on to it, and to go out and put your trust in another person or situation again. It's true that this leaves you open to the possibility of being hurt again, but without this vulnerability, you may never get close to someone or take any kind of risk again. This would not only erode your confidence but also your general levels of life satisfaction. Allowing someone to get close to you only feels special and valuable because you're vulnerable. So remember that every person and situation is different and trust in yourself that not only do you know your boundaries better this time around but that you also know you can handle it.

> Remember that every person and situation is different

Do you see the value and logic in this but still feel a little stuck on how to let go and move forward? Have a look at the following list and try out the tips that feel relevant to you.

Letting go

- Give yourself an amount of time to just feel the pain. Don't fight it and allow yourself to really wallow in it if you like! But with a deadline

- If you find yourself ruminating after the deadline has past, realise that a lot of the painful feelings are now triggered in response to your own thoughts. It's not the other person doing it to you anymore. It's you!

- Accept that it happened. It can't be undone!

- Don't ask why. Demanding an explanation from someone can be pointless as they may not know why they behaved that way themselves. And if the person is no longer around to ask, the 'why' questions will keep you prisoner. Let go of them and accept what has happened

- If it's about someone you've chosen to keep in your life, establish an agreed contract. Basically, this involves one person promising not to repeat their behaviour, while the other agrees to leave it in the past. There'll always be trigger points that remind you of the pain – establish a way to discuss how you feel when they occur

- Accept an apology. When you're upset, you may suspect someone of faking their apology, or of just saying the words to get things back on track. Try to accept the apology – think of it as the crucial platform from which your own confidence can grow and from which further communication can develop.

Once a person knows that you accept their regret is genuine, you can start to rebuild the relationship. This also reduces the risk of repeat offences

- Accept the lack of an apology. When someone isn't around anymore, or it's a relationship which has ended, there may not be an apology. When you find it within yourself to still let go and move on you'll enjoy greater peace of mind. When you don't, the other person is still in control

- Accept vulnerability. As discussed above, it can be very hard feeling vulnerable to future betrayal as there's no guarantee you won't be hurt again. However vulnerability is key to intimacy and closeness so try to see it as necessary to mending a relationship. It's also key to your own progress and growth as it will always involve a level of risk taking. If you're always wondering 'what if?', you won't be able to get close or take risks again

- Accept uncertainty. There are never any guarantees of circumstances remaining the same or of someone continuing to behave in a certain way. Anyone might do something hurtful to us in the future. The only thing that is guaranteed is our own loneliness and lack of confidence if we don't allow that risk in our lives

Ultimately this is about looking to the future rather than dwelling on the past and enjoying the relief and confidence which follow.

You might also want to take a look at "I'm discriminated against" for more about how our beliefs can shape our reality.

I'm discriminated against

Are you a woman in a man's world, black in a white world, gay in a straight world or part of another minority group?

A perception that you're being discriminated against may of course be justified. However, if you allow this to affect your confidence, it might become a self-fulfilling prophecy because your own behaviour could help to create the outcome you are expecting.

Let's explore this. Imagine you are looking for a new job and a great opportunity comes along. Then you hesitate to apply, as you feel pretty certain that however qualified you are for the role, your minority status will be a barrier to you getting the job. So you don't apply, immediately making it a reality that you do not get the job. A negative self-fulfilling prophecy at its most obvious!

Or you *do* apply but when you get to the interview your lack of confidence based on your expectations of discrimination makes you feel nervous, intimidated or like 'there's no point in bothering'.

In this scenario, do you think you're likely to perform at the same level as another candidate who believes they'd be perfect for the job? Their enthusiasm and attitude is certainly likely to beat yours and they will succeed in getting the job. But is that necessarily down to discrimination? Is it the fault of the recruiter? After all, they are there to hire the best match and will reasonably pick the person who most effectively demonstrated that. The only reason you didn't demonstrate that was because of your own beliefs about discrimination, not because of *actual* discrimination.

In this scenario you made it a reality that you did not get the job. Another fully fledged negative self-fulfilling prophecy.

This is not to say there aren't circumstances in which people *are* discriminated against. We know it does unfortunately still go on. Hence your negative expectations in the first place.

However you can minimise the chances of these types of situation arising by avoiding making it easier for people to rule you out. Whether deliberate discrimination is part of the actual motivation or not, make it tough for people to say no to you. In whichever scenario you find yourself.

Be aware of how your own behaviour can affect outcomes and make sure you give yourself the best chance. Here's a technique you can try out:

Acting 'as if'

When you enter a situation you feel insecure about you will, consciously or not, be sending out negative or self-conscious signals to those around you, making it more likely that the outcome will indeed be negative. What happens here is the following:

Negative expectation ➢ Self-defeating behaviour ➢ Poor outcome

Of course, your insecurities come from experiences (your own or others' that you know about) so you're not simply going to be able to switch on confidence, but you are in control of what people see and the version of you that they see. So replace the self-defeating behaviour by acting 'as if' you're confident/the best candidate/the one to listen to/whatever applies best to your situation:

Negative expectation ➢ Act 'as if' ➢ Improved outcome

The outcome is only improved because you're acting, and you may slip up at times. But over time, as positive outcomes add up, you'll prove yourself wrong, your expectations will change and the acting will be replaced with actual confident behaviour:

Positive expectation ➢ Confident behaviour ➢ Good outcome

The outcome will get better and better as your confidence grows and other people's prejudices will no longer affect you.

Notice however how I refer to the outcome as 'good' rather than 'perfect' or even 'great', as it's still possible you'll be disappointed at some point in the future. But that shouldn't feed negative expectations. There is no such thing as perfection.

This is an effective technique to use at any time when your lack of confidence is threatening to get in your way, even when discrimination isn't part of your experience.

Obviously this technique will not protect you from genuine discrimination, however it *will* ensure you don't help those wishing to discriminate against you by performing poorly. You'll also be less likely to sense discrimination where none exists.

See also how to mimic a role model in "I was born

negative" for more ideas on acting 'as if', and read about the importance of your body language on your success in "I'm an introvert".

Life

I have too much on my plate

Do you feel you never have enough time to fit every-thing in or to do anything properly?

It's true that life is busy. Technology has increased the pace at which we live our lives, leaving us feeling overloaded and dissatisfied. We can then end up blaming ourselves for not achieving more in the time we have available and fail to acknowledge the successes we do achieve. We lose sight of how to be calm and peaceful, how to know that we are OK and how we are enough.

It's true that life is busy

One of my clients had a busy family life alongside a successful career and though she appeared to be on top of it all, and others often expressed how in awe they were of how she was managing to spin so many plates, she herself felt drained, insecure, like she never accomplished enough and like she was always waiting for things to calm down. I'd often hear her say things like, 'When the eldest has gone off to university….', 'When I have trained up my new PA…', 'When my daughter is old enough to cycle to school....' and all along, she was self-critical and not confident about her ability to cope.

The fact is no one gets everything done in this day and age. There is no end of things we think we need to get done. Rarely do we get to the bottom of our In Tray. There's always another phone call to make, another dinner to cook, more clothes to iron or another event to attend. And unless you accept that this is reality, regardless of how much you do achieve you'll never feel satisfied or at ease.

But this feeling of not being up to the task originates with you. Life happens around you and it's your response to its demands that dictates your level of confidence. Life can be busy but you don't have to react with negative feelings of not being or doing enough.

In other words, if the above rings a bell for you, you can change it with a shift of focus. Because an overly busy life doesn't have to be an excuse and the missing link to living and enjoying your life with self-confidence is *you*.

To accomplish this shift you'll need to develop ways of blocking out mental clutter so that you can deal with what is in front of you at the time – mindfulness is an effective way of doing this.

Mindfulness originates from the East and its benefits have been recognised there for thousands of years. The practices used there are typically very time consuming and often linked with religious beliefs that may not fit so well with our more secular society but in recent years, mindfulness practices have been adapted to our Western way of life and are gaining momentum.

Here's a mindfulness practice you can try, to introduce some calm into your life:

Being more mindful

Focus on your breathing for 5 minutes. Close your eyes if you wish, and really take notice of the air streaming in and out of your nose. Feel how it's colder coming in and warmer coming out. Really empty your lungs before your next deep breath. Try to simply focus on the act of breathing and when other thoughts come into your mind gentle bring yourself back to it. Your thoughts *will* stray, so don't give yourself a hard time about it, simply notice it when it happens (this can also take a little while, especially at the beginning) and bring yourself back to the breathing. Over time it'll become easier and easier, and as you get used to the stillness and focus of this exercise, try increasing the time you spend doing it. Equally, if two or three minutes feels like all you can fit in and/or have the peace of mind to do, that's fine too. Try increasing when you're able to and allow yourself to be pleased with whatever you manage. Try doing this exercise daily and you can do it as many times as you are able to and feel like in any given day. You'll soon notice a greater ability to maintain a calm and positive perspective and deal with daily challenges.

If you're interested in finding out more about mindfulness I've included some recommendations for further reading in the bibliography at the back of this book.

Acknowledge the things you do achieve

In addition to adopting a calmer approach you could also work on accepting that you don't *have* to get everything done *all* of the time. Instead, acknowledge the things you do achieve. Notice the things you *do*, rather than the ones you don't. Take a look at "No one appreciates me" for advice on how to keep a daily success diary.

I'm tired all the time

Does feeling tired make you doubt yourself and your decisions?

There are times in life when tiredness is inevitable. When we have a new baby or are working towards a challenging work deadline perhaps. It's your peace of mind that is important here. Accept that you'll have to cope with less sleep for a while. Be aware that your current situation is temporary. The worrying you may otherwise experience could be more exhausting than the lack of sleep itself!

There are also times when we choose to sleep less – maybe all the social events around Christmas or lots of summer barbecue invitations. However no one forces us to attend them all. So rather than simply saying 'yes' to every invitation you can choose to make more conscious decisions based on your own wellbeing.

If work worries keep you awake at night or you get stuck in the office late into the evenings, you have a choice whether it's worth it or not. As hard as it may be, changing your job or even your career is possible, and could be advisable if your wellbeing is being negatively affected. You just need to make a decision and act on it.

There are always going to be times when sleep will be more elusive than we'd wish but there are many ways in which you can increase your chances of a good night's sleep. Here are some examples you might like to try:

- Watch some TV before bedtime. After a busy day this can help you switch off

- Do NOT watch TV in the bedroom. In fact, leave all technology outside of the bedroom. It's amazing how your brain will stay alert when faced with a screen of some kind. And particularly the interactive kind. You wouldn't fall asleep mid-conversation in real life and you're not likely to when communicating on social media

- Read a book in bed before turning the light off. You may find this will make your eyelids heavy quite quickly, and at the very least it's likely to free your mind from the daily clutter

- Make up if necessary – upset feelings are a sure way to stay awake!

- Brain dump – if your to-do list is swirling around in your head, write it down so you know you won't forget and then relax. You may want to keep a pad and pen by your bed for this

- Breathe! Paying attention to your breathing calms your mind and relaxes your body and will make it easier to drift off

- Focus on the present. Try not to reflect about events in the past or worry about things to come by focusing on the here and now. Again, your breathing is a good thing on which to focus, or just sense your different body parts against the mattress or listen to the night noises in your bedroom. Bring your attention to the present

- If you wake at night feeling worried or anxious, smile, and allow the positive emotions that follow to act as a calming effect (see "I'm an introvert" for more about the positive effects of smiling)

- Make sure your room is dark, quiet and not too hot

- Avoid caffeine in the evenings, and even during the afternoons if you're sensitive to its effect

- Avoid alcohol as it can prevent a peaceful night's sleep

When your sleep improves you'll find that you have more physical and emotional energy to invest in yourself, and your confidence levels should improve as a result.

Some Final Thoughts

So you've now learnt how to trust yourself and your own ability to handle things, set goals, think more positively, be kind to yourself and notice your own strengths and achievements.

Below you will find some final pointers on how to take this forward, to ensure the greatest success in your quest for greater confidence and to make sure you achieve your confidence on *your* terms, in ways that suit *you!*

Pick the right time for *you*

We tend to think that there are 'good' times to make changes or improvements to our lives. The most common one is the beginning of a new year. We've been brainwashed to think of it in terms of 'now or never' (or at least until next January, a whole year away!) However, it's important to recognise that the 'New Year, New You' concept is an entirely artificial social tradition.

Likewise, some people get stuck on the fact that changes have to start at the beginning of a week. So if it's midweek and you feel bad about something you did or didn't do, for instance standing up to your boss, being honest with your partner or treating yourself in a kind and positive way, you postpone actions to improve the situation until the following week. Fresh start on Monday!

Similar self-imposed 'perfect' times might be after Easter or after the Summer holidays.

Does this ring a bell with you?

If so, you're wasting days, weeks or months feeling bad whilst continuing with behaviour which isn't serving you well, waiting for your fresh start.

Who is in control here?

Strangely, the calendar! A physical thing, with no desires, motivations or real power and that has nothing to do with how you lead your life.

In fact maybe next Monday, the beginning of next year or after your next holiday would be terrible times for you. Then consider what would be a better time.

Who is in control here?

If you feel more energised or motivated when the sun is shining, around a certain anniversary, when a big deadline has passed or after a big event, use that in your plan.

Don't wait for the perfect time

Hopefully you'll now understand that the *perfect* time simply doesn't exist. Be honest with yourself. Is the benefit of putting something off greater than that of achieving your ambitions? If the answer is yes then, fine, it's your prerogative to put it off. But nothing will change until you do.

So whilst you should pick the *right* time for you, don't wait for the perfect one!

Notice what you have already

People often focus on what they feel is missing in their lives. However, by focusing on what's missing you're not acknowledging or appreciating what you already have. I often ask what's the point of working hard, being sociable, living healthily, being a good parent, partner, friend and so on if all you notice is the one thing you didn't get around to doing or which you didn't get 100% right? How come that one thing is worthy of more attention than the stuff you have achieved, or did get right? If you stay focused on what you don't have, what you failed at or what you dislike about yourself, that's what you'll get. Shift your attention to what you *do* have, what you *have* achieved and what you enjoy and more will follow as your confidence grows. Your choice!

Don't compare

Your strengths, your successes, the lovely things and people in your life are no less because someone else has more. Someone else will always have more. That's a given. So the fact that your neighbour, friend or sibling earns more, or is more outgoing, thinner, has more friends or a thriving career doesn't reduce the value of *your* achievements or self-worth. Often, our autopilot response is to think that our good stuff isn't that good when someone else has more, which is guaranteed to damage our confidence. Yet I'm sure you admire many people who aren't world champions. Being the best is not necessary to feeling pride or having others' admiration and, importantly, it's not necessary for being confident in yourself, your abilities and achievements.

Shift your attention to what you *do* have

Don't be a victim

We can all think of times when we did our best and things still didn't go to plan. We can all think of situations when circumstances or other people made our lives harder. This is not unique to any of us. Yet it can be easy to use these people or circumstances as an excuse for not getting our act together and not getting on with whatever we know we need and want to achieve. Who's in control of your life then? That other person or situation? Take the control back, think about how *you* can improve things and where *you* can take more responsibility. Don't wait for other people to act.

If you can put these suggestions into practice you'll begin to feel more empowered, energised and, most importantly, more confident.

Only *you* can build your own confidence. Make it happen for yourself and reap the benefits.

About the Author

Charlotta has been coaching professionally for over 15 years and in 2013 she won Life Coach of the Year, awarded by the national body Association of Professional Coaches, Trainers and Consultants.

Her background is within Human Resources and she started her busy coaching practice, Be Me Life Coaching, in January 2007.

Charlotta specialises in confidence, direction and entrepreneur coaching and she delivers motivational talks and workshops that encourage personal and professional success.

After 19 years in England Charlotta is now living in her native country Sweden together with her British husband and two young children. She regularly travels to the UK for her work.

Find out more at:
www.bemelifecoaching.com
Email: charlotta@bemelifecoaching.com
Phone: +44 (0)7720 839773
Facebook: www.facebook.com/bemelifecoaching.com
Twitter: @charlottahughes
Instagram: charlottahughes

Acknowledgements

My biggest thank you goes to my family.

It's been a real team effort, especially as I've written this book during my maternity leave for our second child.

I've spent many of Henry's napping hours typing away, so my first thanks go to him for being such a good sleeper.

Our 6-year old Emilie has been the best big sister, entertaining her brother when I've had to respond to the editor or finish off a piece when he wakes. She's also given me all important balance with lots of fun and play through the months.

I'm so grateful to my mother-in-law Ray Hughes, whose endless love for and enthusiastic play with both Henry and Emilie have allowed me precious opportunities to leave the house and really focus on my work. Her efficient and quick proof-reading was also invaluable.

A big thank you goes to my husband David. Without his flexibility around his own work, giving me the peace and space to write, this book would not yet be a reality. He's always my most important confidant and I'm eternally grateful for his continual belief in me and his enthusiasm for my many ideas and thoughts.

Last but not least, thanks to Joanne Henson for

giving me this great opportunity and for the interesting and fun editing process through which she's led me.

Reference/ Bibliography

Pauline R Clance, The Imposter Phenomenon: Overcoming the Fear That Haunts Your Success
Peachtree, 1985

Dr Amy Cuddy, Your Body Language Shapes Who You Are http://www.ted.com/talks/amy_cuddy_your_body_language_shapes_who_you_are

Robert Emmons, Thanks! How Practicing Gratitude Can Make You Happier
Mariner Books, 2008

Christopher K Gerber, The Mindful Path to Self-Compassion: Freeing Yourself from Destructive Thoughts and Emotions
Guilford Press, 2009

Susan Jeffers, Feel the Fear and Do it Anyway
Vermilion, 2007

Astrid Lindgren, Pippi Longstocking
Puffin, 2005

Natasha Mann, Benefits of Smiling
http://www.netdoctor.co.uk/healthy-living/bene-
fits-of-smiling.htm

Sandy MacGregor, CALM – Subconscious mind does
not know the difference https://www.youtube.com/
watch?v=jzlxlx87c7k

Kristin Neff, Self Compassion
http://self-compassion.org

Julie Poland, Overcoming the Inner Autopilot
http://thesummitblog.blogspot.se/2010/07/overcom-
ing-inner.html

Harold E Sconier, The Health Benefits of Smiling
http://www.livestrong.com/article/18859-health-bene-
fits-smiling/

The Power of Posture
http://www.economist.com/node/17899714

Other recommended reading

Russ Harris, The Happiness Trap
Robinson, 2008

Paul McGee, SUMO (Shut Up, Move on)
Capstone Publishing Ltd, 2006

Jeffrey M. Schwartz and Sharon Begley – The Mind
and the Brain, Neuroplasticity and the Power of Mental
Force
Regan Books, 2003

Mark Williams and Danny Penman, Mindfulness – An
eight-week plan for Finding Peace in a Frantic World
Macmillan, 2011

Index

Also in this series

What's Your Excuse for not Eating Healthily?

Joanne Henson
Overcome your excuses and eat well to look good and feel great

Do you wish you could eat more healthily and improve the way you look and feel, but find that all too often life gets in the way? Do you regularly embark on healthy eating plans or diets but find that you just can't stick with them? Then this is the book for you.

This isn't another diet book. Instead it's a look at the things which have tripped you up in the past and offers advice, ideas and inspiration to help you overcome those things this time around.

No willpower? Hate healthy food? Got no time to cook? Crave sugary snacks? Overcome all of these excuses and many more. Change your eating habits and relationship with food for good.

Paperback – ISBN 978-0-9933388-2-3
e-book – ISBN 978-0-9933388-3-0

Also in this series

What's Your Excuse for not Living a Life You Love?

Monica Castenetto
Overcome your excuses and lead a happier, more fulfilling life

Are you stuck in a life you don't love? Have you reached a point where your life doesn't feel right for you anymore? Then this book is for you.

This is not yet another self-help book claiming to reveal the secret to permanent happiness. Instead, it helps you to tackle the things which have been holding you back and gives ideas, advice and inspiration to help you move on to a better life.

Don't know what you want? Scared of failure? Hate change? Worried about what others might think? This book will help you overcome all of your excuses and give you the motivation you need to change your life.

Paperback – ISBN 978-0-9933388-4-7
e-book – ISBN 978-0-9933388-5-4

Also in this series

What's Your Excuse for not Loving Your Job?

Amanda Cullen
Overcome your excuses and change the way you feel about your work

Do you have a job which you're not enjoying as much as you know you should? Do you dread Mondays, spend your free time worrying about your work or feel undervalued by your boss or colleagues? If so, this book is for you.

In this supportive and motivational book Amanda Cullen takes a look at the wide variety of excuses we use which keep us stuck and unhappy in our work. She offers ideas and advice on how to tackle issues so that you can take control, make the necessary changes and transform your working life.

Don't like your colleagues? Spend too long in the office? Not confident in your skills? Or just plain bored? Overcome all of these and many more, and learn how to love your job.

Paperback – ISBN 978-0-9933388-6-1
e-book – ISBN 978-0-9933388-7-8

Also in this series

What's Your Excuse for not Getting Fit?

Joanne Henson
Overcome your excuses and get active, healthy and happy

Do you want to be fit, lean and healthy, but find that all too often life gets in the way? Do you own a gym membership you don't use, or take up running every January only to give up in February? Then this is the book for you.

This is not yet another get-fit-quick program. It's a look at the things which have prevented you in the past from becoming the fit, active person you've always wanted to be, and a source of advice, inspiration and ideas to help you overcome those things this time around. Change your habits and attitude to exercise for good.

Too tired? Lacking motivation? Bored by exercise? You won't be after reading this book!

Paperback – ISBN 978-0-9933388-0-9
e-book – ISBN 978-0-9933388-1-6

Also in this series

What's Your Excuse for not Being Better With Money?

Jo Thresher
Overcome your excuses and get to grips with your personal finances

Do you wish you could be savvier with money but find it too daunting? Do you wish you were more in control of your finances but find yourself avoiding taking action? Then this is the book for you.

Personal finance expert Jo Thresher takes a look at all of the reasons you might give for not getting to grips with your money, and offers advice, ideas and inspiration to help you change that.

No time to get organised? Scared to look at your bank statement? Think you're a shopaholic? Not money minded? Overcome all of these excuses and many more. Improve your relationship with your cash and feel more secure, more relaxed and more in control.

Paperback – ISBN 978-0-9956052-0-6
e-book – ISBN 978-0-9956052-1-3